Sally and the leaves

"Here is a red leaf,"

said Sally.

"Here is a yellow leaf,"

said Sally.

"Here is a brown leaf,"

said Sally.

"Look at the leaves!"

said Mum.

"Here is the red leaf,"

said Sally.

"Here is the yellow leaf,"

said Sally.

"Here is the brown leaf," said Sally.

"The leaves are for you, Mum," said Sally.